31 Paleo Meatless Dishes

Quick and Easy Recipes for Side Dishes or Vegetarians

Mary Scott

DISCLAIMER

take responsibility for any consequences that are believed to be a result of following the instructions in this book.

Table of Contents

INTRODUCTION

Vegetables and fruits provide us with an amazing life energy and that is why you will feel absolutely amazing when you try out the recipes in the nature-loving, zen-invoking 31 Paleo Vegetarian Recipes cookbook.

The Paleolithic lifestyle is all about eating clean, wholesome foods like our ancestors did thousands of years ago and there is no better demonstration than delicious veggie recipes
This book is an ode to nature and her creative genius when it comes to all-natural foods and flavor.

Try out delicious salads like the Decadent Avocado and Walnut Salad or sashay to the Far East with Paleo Tabbouleh, after that the fantastic and creamy Artichoke soup is a must-try if you enjoy subtle, delicious flavors. The main selections take you from lunch through to dinner with succulent Red Pepper Pesto Stuffed Mushrooms and Friday night Margherita Pizza Pie or the antioxidant powerhouse Kale and Almond Stir-Fry

If you're trying out Paleo Vegetarian then you must try the desserts. On deck we have super Paleo Vanilla Ice Cream and heavenly Grilled Peaches with Coconut Cream - your guests will be sliding off their chairs in a mutual - Oh Wow! The beauty of Paleo desserts is that you will feel super good as they dance in your mouth and also when you think about them later and realize your dessert was totally Paleo and totally guilt-free.

Paleo eating is about enjoying wholesome foods that nourish your body and soul. Get ready for 31 days of uber delicious vegetarian eats that will change the way you feel about vegging out.

Happy Paleo!

SALADS

Decadent Avocado Walnut Salad
Serves: 4-6
Prep Time: 10 minutes

Ingredients
Salad Base
1 small head romaine lettuce, chopped
1 bell pepper, seeded, julienned
2 avocados, peeled, sliced
1/3 cup walnuts, chopped

Dressing
1 lime, juiced
1/4 cup fresh orange juice
2 tbsp. coconut oil
1 tsp. salt, black pepper

Directions
1. Combine ingredients for dressing and whisk.
2. Combine salad ingredients in large glass bowl and drizzle dressing.

Nutrition (g)
Calories 361
Fat 33
Sodium 597(mg)
Carbs 17
Protein 6

Mediterranean Tabbouleh Salad

Serves: 4 - 6
Prep Time: 20 minutes

Ingredients

Salad Base
1 small head cauliflower
2 tomatoes, chopped
2 cucumbers, diced
2 cups parsley, chopped
1/4 cup green onions, chopped
1/2 cup fresh mint

Dressing
2 lemons, juiced
1/4 cup coconut oil
1/4 tsp. cinnamon, allspice, coriander
1 tsp. salt, black pepper

Directions
1. Mix the dressing together, set aside.
2. Grate the cauliflower so you have rice-like granules and place in large glass bowl.
3. Add remaining salad ingredients, combine well, and mix in dressing.

Nutrition (g)
Calories 186
Fat 14
Sodium 628 (mg)
Carbs 14
Protein 4

Raspberry Spinach Salad with Warm Poppy Seed Dressing

Serves: 4
Prep Time: 10 minutes

Ingredients

Salad Base
6 cups spinach
1 cup raspberries
1/4 cup cashew, chopped

Dressing
2 tbsp. ghee
2 tsp. poppy seeds
1/4 tsp. dry mustard
1/2 tsp. salt, black pepper

Directions
1. Heat ghee in saucepan on medium, add remaining ingredients and cook for a minute, set aside.
2. Toss spinach, raspberries, sunflower seeds and drizzle with warm buttery dressing.

Nutrition (g)
Calories 140
Fat 11
Sodium 330 (mg)
Carbs 8
Protein 3

Roasted Squash and Arugula Salad

Serves: 4
Prep Time: 10 minutes

Ingredients

4 cups arugula, stemmed
1 cup flat-leaf parsley
3 cloves garlic, peeled, minced
1 small acorn squash
1 tsp. pine nuts
2 lemons, juiced
1/2 tsp. dry mustard
1 tsp. salt, black pepper
Coconut oil for cooking

Directions

1. Preheat oven to 400 degrees and line roasting tray with parchment paper.
2. Slice squash in half, remove seeds, brush with coconut oil.
3. Place squash face down on roasting tray and place in oven for 45 minutes.
4. Remove from oven, cool and separate flesh from skin.
5. Chop squash into 1" cubes, set aside.
6. In blender, combine parsley, lemon, 4 tbsp. coconut oil, pine nuts, dry mustard, salt, pepper and mix until well combined into chunky dressing.
7. Toss squash with arugula and dressing.

Nutrition (g)
Calories 189
Fat 15
Sodium 599(mg)
Carbs 17
Protein 3

Beet and Walnut Salad

Serves: 4
Prep Time: 15 minutes

Ingredients

8 beets
1 cup flat-leaf parsley, chopped
1/2 cup walnuts
2 tbsp. sesame seeds
2 tbsp. flaxseed
4 slices dried peach, chopped
2 tbsp. balsamic vinegar
1 tsp. salt and pepper

Directions

1. Preheat oven to 400 degrees and line roasting sheet with parchment paper.
2. Place bets on roasting sheet and place in oven for 45 minutes.
3. When baking is complete, remove, peel and cut into thin slices.
4. Toss with balsamic vinegar, salt and pepper, set aside
5. In skillet, heat 2 tbsp. ghee on medium.
6. Add chopped walnuts, sesame seed, flax seed and dried peach, sauté for a minute.
7. In bowl combine parsley, beets and walnut mixture and serve.

Nutrition (g)
Calories 241
Fat 13
Sodium 165 (mg)
Carbs 26
Protein 9

Carrot Cashew Salad

Serves: 4
Prep Time: 10 minutes

Ingredients

4 medium carrots, peeled, shredded
2 cups cilantro, stemmed
1/2 cup cashews, soaked overnight
6 dates, pitted, halved
3 limes, juiced
1/2 tsp. paprika
1 tsp. salt, black pepper
2 tbsp. coconut oil

Directions

1. Combine salt, pepper, paprika, lime juice and coconut oil, set aside.
2. Chop cashews and place in salad bowl, add remaining ingredients, toss.
3. Drizzle with dressing and serve.

Nutrition (g)

Calories 235
Fat 15
Sodium 631 (mg)
Carbs 27
Protein 4

SOUPS

Thai Shiitake Lime Soup
Serves: 4
Prep Time: 20 minutes

Ingredients

1/2 lb. shiitake mushrooms
1/2 cup coconut milk
2 cups low-sodium vegetable stock
2 tbsp. ginger, grated
2 tsp. lemongrass, minced
2 red bell peppers, seeded, sliced
1 onion, peeled, sliced
4 cloves garlic, peeled, minced
2 kaffir lime leaves
2 tsp. salt
1 tsp. black pepper
Coconut oil for cooking

Directions

1. Heat 3 tbsp. coconut oil in skillet; add garlic, onion and sauté until onion is translucent.
2. Add bell peppers and shiitake mushrooms, sauté for another minute.
3. Mix in remaining ingredients, reduce heat to low, cover and simmer for 20 minutes.
4. Remove lime leaves and serve.

Nutrition (g)
Calories 249
Fat 18
Sodium 1385(mg)
Carbs 22
Protein 3

Delicious Broccoli Soup

Serves: 4
Prep Time: 20 minutes

Ingredients

6 cups broccoli florets
2 onions, peeled, diced
4 cloves garlic, minced
2 cups low sodium chicken stock
1 cup almond milk
1 tsp. chives
1 lemon, juiced
1 tsp. red pepper flakes
1 tsp. salt, black pepper
Coconut oil for cooking

Directions

1. In skillet heat 3 tbsp. coconut oil on medium.
2. Add garlic, onion and sauté until onion is translucent.
3. Add broccoli, sauté for 3-4 minutes, add salt, pepper, chives.
4. Stir in liquids and bring to boil.
5. Cover and reduce heat to medium low for 15 minutes.
6. Using hand immersion blender, mix until smooth.

7. Ladle into bowls and sprinkle a little red pepper flake on top.

Nutrition (g)
Calories 283
Fat 22
Sodium 670(mg)
Carbs 20
Protein 7

Celery Root, Apple and Walnut Soup

Serves: 4

Prep Time: 10 minutes

Ingredients

1 celery root, peeled,
1 green apple, peeled, cored
1/3 cup walnuts, chopped
1 onion, peeled and diced
1 cup coconut milk
2 tbsp. dill
1 tsp. salt, black pepper
Coconut oil for cooking

Directions

1. Dice celery root and green apple into 1" chunks
2. Heat 3 tbsp. coconut oil in skillet.
3. Add onion and walnut, sauté until onion is translucent.
4. Add celery root, sauté for 3 minutes.
5. Add coconut milk and bring to boil.
6. Reduce heat and simmer for 25 minutes.
7. Using hand immersion blender, mix until smooth.
8. Add apple, reduce heat to low, simmer for 10 minutes.

Nutrition (g)
Calories 346
Fat 31
Sodium 633(mg)
Carbs 17
Protein 5

Creamy Butternut Squash and Pistachio Soup

Serves: 4
Prep Time: 10 minutes

Ingredients

1 butternut squash
1/4 cup pistachio, shelled, chopped
1 onion, peeled, diced
4 cloves garlic, peeled, minced
1 cup coconut milk
4 cups low-sodium vegetable stock
1 tsp. salt, black pepper
Coconut oil for cooking

Directions

1. Preheat oven to 400 degrees, line roasting tray with parchment paper.
2. Chop squash in half, remove seeds and brush with coconut oil.
3. Place squash face down on roasting tray and place in oven for 40 minutes.
4. Remove from oven; remove skin and rough chop flesh.
5. In soup pot, heat 3 tbsp. coconut oil for medium.
6. Add garlic, onion, pistachio and sauté until onion is translucent.

7. Mix in butternut squash pieces and remaining ingredients.
8. Cover, bring to a boil, reduce heat and simmer for 15 minutes.
9. Cool and using immersion blender, blend soup until smooth.

Nutrition (g)
Calories 396
Fat 28
Sodium 1169 (mg)
Carbs 37
Protein 5

Asparagus Soup

Serves: 4
Prep Time: 20 minutes

Ingredients

1 lb. asparagus spears, cut into 1" pieces
2 cups spinach, chopped
2 green onions, chopped
3 cloves garlic, minced
3 cups low-sodium vegetable stock
1 tsp. paprika
1 tsp. salt, black pepper
Coconut oil for cooking

Directions

1. Heat 3 tbsp. coconut oil over medium heat in soup pot.
2. Add garlic, onion, sauté until onion is translucent.
3. Add asparagus and sauté for a minute.
4. Stir in remaining ingredients, cover, bring to boil.
5. Reduce heat, simmer for 20 minutes.
6. Using hand immersion blender, blend soup until smooth.

Nutrition (g)
Calories 128
Fat 10
Sodium 1410 (mg)
Carbs 7
Protein 3

MAIN DISHES

Summer Squash Bake

Serves: 4
Prep Time: 15 minutes

Ingredients

3 yellow squash, sliced
1 zucchini, sliced
1 red onion, peeled, diced
6 cloves garlic, peeled, chopped
1/2 cup, cashews, soaked overnight, chopped
2 lemons, juiced
1 tsp. rosemary
1 tsp. salt, black pepper
Coconut oil for cooking

Directions

1. Preheat oven to 400 degrees and lightly coat an 8" baking dish with coconut oil.
2. Heat 2 tbsp. coconut oil in skillet, sauté until onion is translucent.
3. Place onion mixture in bottom of tray, starting from outside of baking dish. Place zucchini and squash back-to-back vertically like dominoes all the way around tray, make another circle inside the first and place remaining slices in center.

4. Sprinkle with cashew nuts, salt, pepper, thyme and lemon juice.
5. Cover with aluminum foil and place in oven for 35 minutes.

Nutrition (g)
Calories 118
Fat 7
Sodium 603 (mg)
Carbs 14
Protein 3

Garlic Mushroom Curry

Serves: 4
Prep Time: 10 minutes

Ingredients

4 cups wild mushrooms, stemmed
1 onion, peeled, diced
4 cloves garlic, peeled, minced
1 tsp. ginger, peeled, grated
1 cup tomatoes, crushed
1 cup coconut milk
1 tsp. curry powder
1/2 tsp. cumin seeds
1 tsp. salt, black pepper
Coconut oil for cooking

Directions

1. Heat 3 tbsp. coconut oil in soup pot; add garlic onion, sauté until onion is translucent.
2. Add mushrooms, ginger, sauté.
3. Stir in remaining ingredients, bring to boil.
4. Reduce heat to low, cover and simmer for

Nutrition (g)

Calories 209
Fat 18
Sodium 598 (mg)
Carbs 11
Protein 4

Mexican Stuffed Pepper

Serves: 4
Prep Time: 15 minutes

Ingredients

8 yellow bell pepper
1 medium onion, peeled, diced
4 cloves garlic, minced
1 jalapeno pepper, seeded, diced
3 tomatoes, chopped
1 lime, juiced
4 cups cauliflower, grated
1 tsp. oregano, cumin, paprika
1 tsp. salt, black pepper
Coconut oil for cooking

Directions

1. Preheat oven to 375 degrees, place parchment paper on baking sheet.
2. Heat 3 tbsp. oil in skillet; add onion, garlic, sauté until onion is translucent.
3. Add tomatoes, cauliflower, and jalapeno sauté for 5 minutes.
4. Add lime juice, spices, salt, pepper, and stir for another five minutes.
5. Slice tops off bell peppers, remove seeds and place on baking sheet.
6. Spoon skillet mixture into bell peppers, drizzle all with a little coconut oil.
7. Bake for 25 minutes.

Nutrition (g) (two per)
Calories 252
Fat 15
Sodium 626 (mg)
Carbs 28
Protein 6

Middle Eastern Eggplant Dish with Cucumber Discs

Serves: 4
Prep Time: 25 minutes

Ingredients

3 eggplants
2 English cucumbers, sliced
2 onions, peeled, sliced thinly
1/2 cup coconut milk
6 cloves garlic, peeled, minced
1/2 cup walnuts, chopped
1 tsp. salt, black pepper
Coconut oil for cooking

Directions

1. Preheat oven to 400 degrees and place parchment paper on baking sheet.
2. Prick eggplants to make little air holes and place on parchment, roast for 25 minutes.
3. When done turn oven heat down to 375, remove eggplant, mash, set aside.
4. Heat 3 tbsp. of coconut oil in skillet over medium; add garlic onions and sauté until onion translucent.
5. Mix in eggplant, salt, black pepper and coconut milk and cook for 7 minutes, stir intermittently.
6. Sprinkle eggplant with walnut and serve with fresh cucumber discs.

Nutrition (g)
Calories 380
Fat 24
Sodium 598 (mg)
Carbs 40
Protein 10

Margherita Pizza Pie

Serves: 4
Prep Time: 10 minutes

Ingredients

Crust
1-1/2 cup walnuts
2 Medjool Dates, pitted
2 tbsp. ghee

Filling
3 tomatoes, sliced
1 onion, sliced
4 cloves garlic, peeled, minced
4 fresh basil leaves
1/4 cup pine nuts
1 tsp. oregano
1 -1/2 tsp. salt, black pepper

Directions
1. Place walnuts in food processor and crush into meal
2. Add dates, 1/2 tsp. salt, ghee and mix.
3. Spread walnut mixture into an 8" pie plate, pat firmly in place and place in refrigerator for an hour.
4. Preheat oven to 400 degrees.
5. Heat 3 tbsp. coconut oil in skillet over medium; add onion, garlic, sauté until onions are translucent.

6. Add pine nuts and toast for about a minute, add oregano, remaining salt and black pepper
7. Place onion mixture on pie crust, top with tomato slices, basil and a little drizzle of coconut oil.
8. Bake in oven for 25 minutes.

Nutrition (g)
Calories 399
Fat 31
Sodium 587 (mg)
Carbs 32
Protein 11

Curried Sweet Potato and Spinach

Serves: 4

Prep Time: 10 minutes

Ingredients

6 cups spinach, chopped
2 sweet potatoes
2 onions, peeled, sliced
4 cloves garlic, peeled, minced
1 tsp. curry powder
1/4 tsp. cinnamon
1 tsp. salt, black pepper
Coconut oil for cooking

Directions

1. Peel sweet potatoes, chop into 2" bites and place in steamer for 20 minutes
2. Heat 2 tbsp. coconut oil in skillet on medium
3. Add garlic and onions, sauté until onions become translucent.
4. Add spinach, sauté for another minute and mix in spices.
5. Remove sweet potatoes from steamer; add them to skillet and mix.
6. Turn off heat, cover and allow to sit for 10 minutes to allow sweet potatoes to absorb flavors.

Nutrition (g)
Calories 276
Fat 7
Sodium 633 (mg)
Carbs 50
Protein 4

Red Pepper Pesto Stuffed Mushrooms

Serves: 4-6
Prep Time: 10 minutes

Ingredients

2 red bell peppers, seeded, quartered
8 Portobello mushrooms
8 fresh basil leaves
2 tsp. pine nuts
3 cloves garlic, peeled
1 onion, peeled, chopped
1/2 cup cashews, soaked overnight
6 tbsp. coconut oil

Directions

1. Preheat oven to 400 degrees and line baking tray with parchment paper.
2. Place red bell peppers, basil, pine nuts, garlic, onion, coconut oil and cashews in food processor, blend until you have a chunky paste.
3. Place mushrooms on parchment paper, stuff each mushroom with mixture, and bake in oven for 25 minutes.

Nutrition (g)

Calories 362
Fat 30
Sodium 16 (mg)
Carbs 21
Protein 8

Eggplant and Mushroom Lasagna

Serves: 4
Prep Time: 15 minutes

Ingredients

4 medium eggplants
2 tomatoes, diced
2 cups wild mushrooms, sliced
1 red onion, peeled, thinly sliced
4cloves garlic, peeled, finely chopped
1/4 cup parsley, chopped
3 cups organic vegetable stock
1 lemon, juiced
1 tsp. paprika
1 tsp. salt, black pepper
Coconut oil for cooking

Directions

1. Preheat oven to 375 degrees and lightly coat lasagna dish with coconut oil.
2. Cut eggplant into 1/2" vertical slices (like lasagna noodles), set aside.
3. In skillet, heat 3 tbsp. coconut oil over medium, add onions and garlic, stir until onion is translucent.
4. Add tomatoes, stock, salt, pepper, paprika, cover and cook for 20 minutes on low.
5. Spoon a little tomato sauce on bottom of a lasagna dish, place eggplant noodles so they are completely covering the bottom of the dish, ladle some sauce over top of the

noodles followed by a layer of mushrooms, repeating the layering process until either the dish is full or the ingredients are used.

6. Cover dish with aluminum foil and cook for 45 minutes.
7. Serve topped with a sprinkle of parsley.

Nutrition (g)
Calories 246
Fat 8
Sodium 707 (mg)
Carbs 41
Protein 8

Spinach and Roasted Tomatoes

Serves: 4
Prep Time: 15 minutes.

Ingredients

8 cups spinach, chopped
4 tomatoes, quartered
1 onion, peeled, sliced
1/4 cup currants, chopped
4 garlic cloves, minced
1 tsp. oregano,
2 tsp. salt, black pepper
Coconut oil for cooking

Directions

1. Preheat oven to 400 degrees and lightly coat roasting pan with coconut oil.
2. Place tomatoes on pan drizzle with coconut oil, sprinkle with 1/2 tsp. salt and black pepper.
3. Place in oven for 20 minutes.
4. In skillet heat 4 tbsp. coconut oil over medium, add garlic, onions, sauté until onion is translucent.
5. Add currants and spinach; continue to cook until spinach is wilted. Turn off heat and let it rest for 10 minutes.
6. Plate spinach and top with roasted tomatoes.

Nutrition (g)
Calories 145
Fat 11
Sodium 1219 (mg)
Carbs 12
Protein 3

Broccoli Mushroom Stir-Fry with Carrots

Serves: 4

Prep Time: 20 minutes.

Ingredients

3 cups broccoli florets
2 cups button mushrooms, stemmed
4 scallions, sliced
2 tbsp. ginger, grated
4 cloves garlic, minced
1/4 cup walnuts
4 carrots, peeled, grated
1 tsp. black pepper
1 tsp. red pepper flakes
6 tbsp. coconut aminos
Coconut oil for cooking

Directions

1. Heat 4 tbsp. coconut oil in wok.
2. Add onions, garlic, stir-fry a minute.
3. Add mushrooms broccoli florets, stir-fry for three minutes.
4. Add ginger, walnuts, 4 tbsp. coconut aminos, salt, black pepper, and mix well.
5. Turn heat off and cover.
6. Combine grated carrots, with 2 tbsp. coconut aminos and pepper flakes.
7. Plate carrots and top with broccoli and mushroom stir-fry.

Nutrition (g)
Calories 215
Fat 15
Sodium 237 (mg)
Carbs 17
Protein 6

Asian Cabbage Ginger Stir Fry

Serves: 4-6
Prep Time: 20 minutes.

Ingredients

3 carrots, peeled, shredded
1 small head cabbage, shredded
2 red bell pepper, seeded, julienned
1 scallion, chopped
2 tbsp. ginger, grated
2 tbsp. sunflower seeds
1/4 cup walnuts, chopped
2 limes, juiced
3 tbsp. coconut aminos
1 tbsp. black pepper
Coconut oil for cooking

Directions

1. Heat 4 tbsp. coconut oil in wok, add scallion, stir-fry for 30 seconds.
2. Add carrots, cabbage and bell pepper, stir fry for 5 minutes, add ginger and cook for another 2 minutes.
3. Remove from heat, stir in coconut aminos, lime juice, black pepper.
4. Top with walnuts, sunflower seeds and serve.

Nutrition (g)
Calories 245
Fat 16
Sodium 153 (mg)
Carbs 24
Protein 6

Braised Kale with Almonds

Serves: 4
Prep Time: 15 minutes

Ingredients

1 lb. kale, stemmed, rough-chopped
1 cup almonds, soaked overnight, peeled
1 onion, peeled, diced
4 cloves garlic, peeled, minced
1/2 cup vegetable stock
1 tsp. rosemary
1-1/2 tsp. salt, black pepper
Coconut oil for cooking

Directions

1. Heat 3 tbsp. coconut oil in skillet over medium, add garlic, onion and cook until garlic is fragrant.
2. Add kale, sauté for five minutes, add almonds, vegetable stock, and rosemary, salt, pepper, and cook for another five minutes.
3. Remove from heat; allow to rest for a few minutes before serving.

Nutrition (g)
Calories 271
Fat 19
Sodium 644 (mg)
Carbs 21
Protein 9

Flax Seed Wrap

Serves: 2
Prep Time: 10 minutes

Ingredients

1/2 cup flaxseed, ground
2 eggs
1/4 tsp. baking powder
1/2 tsp. salt
2 tbsp. ghee

Directions

1. Whip eggs, add flaxseed, baking powder, salt and mix well.
2. Heat a tablespoon of ghee in skillet and pour in half the batter.
3. Cook for about 2 minutes, flip and cook for another 2 minutes.
4. Add the remaining ghee and the rest of the batter to make the next wrap.

Nutrition (g)

Calories 324
Fat 26
Sodium 652 (mg)
Carbs 9
Protein 11

Almond Tortilla

Serves: 4
Prep Time: 10 minutes

Ingredients

1 cup almond flour
1 egg
1/2 tsp. salt
1 tbsp. coconut oil

Directions

1. Preheat oven to 375 degrees.
2. Whip egg and slowly combine almond flour, salt and coconut oil.
3. Divide dough into four sections rolling each into balls.
4. Place parchment paper on flat surface roll ball out to make a round tortilla.
5. Place another parchment sheet on top and repeat with three remaining balls.

Nutrition (g)

Calories 426
Fat 36
Sodium 632 (mg)
Carbs 12
Protein 15

Artichoke and Caper Wrap

Serves: 6
Prep Time: 10 minutes

Ingredients

6 artichokes, trimmed
2 tsp. capers, rinsed
2 onions, peeled, diced
1 cup parsley, stemmed, chopped
1 lemon, juiced
1 tsp. salt, black pepper
1-1/2 cups arugula, chopped
Coconut oil for cooking
4 flaxseed Wraps

Directions

1. Quarter artichokes and remove exterior.
2. Bring water to boil in pot, add artichokes and half a lemon; continue to boil for 5 minutes, slice artichoke hearts into 1/2" pieces.
3. Add 2 tbsp. coconut oil to skillet, sauté onions, until translucent.
4. Add capers and artichoke hearts, sauté for five minutes.
5. Drizzle with lemon juice and sprinkle with salt and pepper.
6. Line flax seed wrap with arugula and top with artichoke hearts.

Nutrition (g) (Filling)
Calories 208
Fat 7
Sodium 862 (mg)
Carbs 33
Protein 9

Rainbow Pepper and Jalapeno Fajita

Serves: 4
Prep Time: 10 minutes

Ingredients

1 red bell pepper, seeded, julienned
1 yellow bell pepper, seeded, julienned
1 green bell pepper, seeded, julienned
1 tomato, diced
1 onion, peeled, sliced
1 jalapeno, seeded, chopped
4 cloves garlic, peeled, minced
1 tomato, chopped
1 tsp. cumin, oregano
1/2 tsp. paprika
1 tsp. salt, black pepper
Coconut oil for cooking
4 Almond Wraps or Tortillas

Directions

1. In a bowl combines raw tomatoes, lemon juice, 1/2 tsp. salt and spices, set aside.
2. Heat 3 tbsp. coconut oil in skillet over medium heat.
3. Add onions, garlic, sauté until onion is translucent.
4. Add bell peppers jalapeno and sauté until tender.
5. Sprinkle with black pepper and 1/2 tsp. salt.
6. Spoon peppers into almond wrap, top with tomatoes and roll into wrap.

Nutrition (g) (Filling)
Calories 111
Fat 7
Sodium 588 (mg)
Carbs 11
Protein 2

DESSERTS

Vanilla Bean Shake

Serves: 2
Prep Time: 5 minutes

Ingredients

1 banana
3/4 cup coconut cream
3/4 cup ice
1 vanilla bean

Directions

1. Remove beans from the vanilla pods, place beans in blender.
2. Add remaining ingredients and mix until well combined.

Nutrition (g)

Calories 133
Fat 11
Sodium 8 (mg)
Carbs 9
Protein 1

Grilled Peaches with Coconut Cream

Serves: 4-6
Prep Time: 10 minutes

Ingredients

4 peaches, pitted
1 tsp. vanilla bean pods, crushed
1/2 cup coconut cream
1 banana
Coconut oil for cooking

Directions

1. Place banana, coconut cream and vanilla bean in blender and mix until smooth.
2. Heat grill to medium high and brush with a little coconut oil.
3. Slice each peach into eight slices; grill each side for 3 minutes.
4. Plate peaches with a dollop of coconut cream.

Nutrition (g)

Calories 195
Fat 14
Sodium 5 (mg)
Carbs 18
Protein 2

Apple Cinnamon Cashew Pie

Serves: 4
Prep Time: 20 minutes

Ingredients

Crust
1-1/4 cup raw cashews
1/2 cup pecans
2 Medjool dates, pitted, chopped
1/2 tsp. salt

Filling
4 red apples
2 Medjool dates, chopped
½ tsp. vanilla bean pods, crushed
½ tsp. cinnamon

Directions

1. Preheat oven to 350 degrees.
2. Place nuts for crust in food processor and crush until slightly mealy, leave a few chunks for texture.
3. Add dates and salt and mix until well combined.
4. Place in 9" pie dish and place in the refrigerator for an hour.
5. Peel apples, remove seeds, slice.

6. Place apples in a circular pattern in pie plate, sprinkle with dates, cinnamon and crushed vanilla bean.
7. Bake in oven for 20 minutes.

Nutrition (g)
Calories 284
Fat 19
Sodium 296 (mg)
Carbs 27
Protein 7

Vanilla Ice Cream

Serves: 8

Prep Time: 20 minutes

Ingredients

1 cup coconut milk
2 cups coconut cream
1/2 cup raw honey
1 tsp. vanilla extract
1 tbsp. arrowroot starch
1 tsp. whiskey
1 tsp. salt

Directions

1. Combine 1/2 cup coconut milk with arrowroot starch, set aside.
2. Combine 1/2 cup coconut milk, coconut cream and honey in saucepan and place over medium heat, until it begins to come to simmer. Whisk in arrowroot starch mixture, whiskey and bring back up to simmer.
3. Pour coconut mixture into a sealable container, mix in vanilla bean powder, cover and place in refrigerator for 6 hours.
4. Remove and churn in ice cream maker.
5. Transfer ice cream base to a freezer-safe container and freeze for 4 hours.

Nutrition (g)
Calories 278
Fat 22
Sodium 305 (mg)
Carbs 23
Protein 2

CONCLUSION

When vegetables, fruits and nuts are left to shine on their own, they do magical things. The starring elements pop with flavor and provide a freshness that will leave you feeling good all over. Try eating dishes from this book for a few days back-to-back and not only will you be well-satiated but you will also feel a new energy.

The substitution of nuts for grains may seem fat-heavy, but remember you are consuming good fats that your body needs. All of the fat in the nuts is balanced out by your veggies and fruits, which provide ample servings of vitamins, minerals and other nutrients that you may not get when you consume veggies in small side dish portions.

Once you try out some of these recipes you will see that it is quite possible to use vegetables to make traditionally meaty dishes without losing richness and flavor. Your Paleo pizza pie and Eggplant, Mushroom Lasagna will definitely have your family doing a double take on Veggie Paleo.

Enjoy these dishes, share them with your family and friends and use them as inspiration to make whimsical vegetarian Paleo recreations of own.

Happy Veggie Paleo month!

Made in the USA
Middletown, DE
24 March 2016